Rapid Reading Series

Chloe Watches TV
Book 20

Written by G. Grafi
©2021

For Betty:
You have taken on the role of
everyone's mother. It is you
who keeps the family together.

A note to parents and teachers:
This is the twentieth and final
book in the Rapid Reading series.
Its purpose is to practice the
words with silent letters.

In order to read words with silent
letters, one must ignore the silent
letter and read the words without
the sounds of those letters.

The following book contains pages
filled with words with silent
letters that are highlighted for
easier reading.

Follow the guide and use the
tables on the next two pages to
practice the silent letter words
prior to reading the book in order
to facilitate the reading process.

Dr. G. Grafi

Table of Silent Sounds

Silent h	Chloe, school, stomach, chameleon, zucchini characters
Silent t	Margot, witch, castle, beret, ballet, listens, catch, match
Silent k	Knox, knows, knead, knit, knock, knob
Silent r	Wren, wrapping, wrist, wrestled, wrong, wring
Silent l	calm, calf, walk, could, talk, should, half, yolk, would
Silent n	hymn, autumn, column, solemn

Table of Silent Sounds

Silent b	plumber, climb, lamb, thumb, comb
Silent u	guitar, guest, disguise, guessed, biscuits, guilty
Silent g	reigning, gnome, designed, signing, gnat
Silent h	hour, honestly, honored, heir
Silent w	swords, towards, two, answer
Silent w (with wh words)	whole, whose, who (tip: Whenever there is an "o" after a "wh" word, the "w" will always be silent.)

This is Chloe.

Chloe didn't go to school
because her stomach hurt.

Chloe stayed home with
her pet chameleon and
ate zucchini.

Chloe watched TV and saw many characters.

First, she saw Margot, a witch in a castle whose cat wears a beret and loves the ballet.

She listens to music and plays a catch match.

Second, she saw Knox.
He knows how to knead.
Knox also knows how to knit.

Knox hears a knock on the
door and turns the knob.

Third, she saw Wren wrapping
her wrist because she wrestled.

It felt wrong to wring the
cloth.

Then, Chloe saw two swords coming towards each other.

Who were the two fighters?

She didn't know the answer.

Next, she saw a calm calf walk like he could, talk like he should not, and eat a half of a yolk like he would eat it all.

After that, he saw a hymn on
TV in an autumn background
between two columns with a
solemn song on.

Chloe also saw a plumber climb a ladder.

The plumber saw a lamb
and hurt his thumb because
of his comb.

Later, Chloe saw a guitar player as a guest in disguise.

He guessed that he ate too many biscuits and felt guilty.

Much later, she saw the reigning queen next to a gnome in a beautifully designed office.

She was signing a paper while a gnat was buzzing around.

Afterwards, Chloe saw that a whole pizza pie was eaten.

She didn't know whose pizza it was or who ate the whole pizza pie.

Finally, the hour was late, and
Chloe was honestly tired.

Chloe went to sleep and dreamed that she was an honored heir to the throne.

Table of Silent Sounds- Review

Silent h	Chloe, school, stomach, chameleon, zucchini characters
Silent t	Margot, witch, castle, beret, ballet, listens, catch, match
Silent k	Knox, knows, knead, knit, knock, knob
Silent r	Wren, wrapping, wrist, wrestled, wrong, wring
Silent l	calm, calf, walk, could, talk, should, half, yolk, would
Silent n	hymn, autumn, column, solemn

Table of Silent Sounds- Review

Silent b	plumber, climb, lamb, thumb, comb
Silent u	guitar, guest, disguise, guessed, biscuits, guilty
Silent g	reigning, gnome, designed, signing, gnat
Silent h	hour, honestly, honored, heir
Silent w	swords, towards, two, answer
Silent w (with wh words)	whole, whose, who (tip: Whenever there is an "o" after a "wh" word, the "w" will always be silent.)